#WERATECATS

PROFESSIONAL CAT RATINGS BY A CRAZY CAT LADY

FRANKI MILLER

D1293418

ISBN: 978-0-578-64277-2

This is Mr. Dumbles. He is 13 years old. His dreams are to be an outside panther roaming in the jungle, but he has settled to be a house panther spoiled by treats daily. 13/10 handsome VOID

06.05.2011

This is Skittles. He was dumped in the woods as a kitten, very spicy, but turned to be the biggest lover. He is over the rainbow bridge now and is missed dearly. 17/10 Would have loved to pet the belleh. Climb High angel

This is Gregory. He is 10 and the boss of the house. Everyone knows it. He's a little bit of a snob, but will want all the attention when it comes to it as he gets a little jealous of his brother and sister. 13/10 we all want love Greggy it's ok

This is Gingie. He is a softy little cheeto boy is about 10. He is a lil'
baby who has the louder purr you could ever hear, an extreme love bug
with his big belly who loves everyone who comes round. 14/10 I
would walk through boiling hot lava for Gingie

This is Zero. He is a wild house panther who enjoys judging his hoomans while they scoop his litterbox. 11/10 true definition of a VOID.

This is Sherpa Tensing. (2005-2016) She was a beautiful and wise, with an awesome headbonk for the ones she loved and disdain for pretty much everything else. she was gone too young to cancer. 17/10 Climb High sweet girl. Forever floofy angel

This is Bug. He is 4 years old and a foster fail. He has IBD and skin allergies but doesn't let it change his happy-go-lucky outlook on life. 13/10 LIVE UR BEST LIFE BUG. FABULOUS

This is Ernest. He is a senior rescue that was formerly abused for being too loud and now Siamese-yodels to his heart's content in the nice echo-y bathroom at 2 AM. Good thing his adopter is partially deaf and misses most of the midnight operas. 12/10 boy has got PIPES! Would pay to see him in concert

This is Olive. She is 4 and really enjoys chews on electrical cables. Also has dreams of becoming an astronaut. 15/10 weird flex but Olive I support you.

This is Franki. She is the Queen of the #WeRateCats household. Her astrological sign is Leo, so she knows what she wants and will make sure you know it too. Only loves a few specific people and will do anything of tuna. 14/10 please bend the knee for the Q U E E N.

This is Miss Jackie Chan. You may call her Miss Jackie because hoomans are easily offended. Miss Jackie is 8 years old and knows she is fabulous and owns it. 14/10 Miss Jackie you need write a self help book

This is Mitty. She was found in a bag by the water and now hunts among the orchids for flies or naps in the sunshine. She is feared all around by small winged creatures except for the birds. The birds live outside where there's dust and pollen that she's allergic to. Would rather sleep in the window. 15/10 She wants to be a bird. If she's a bird, I'm a bird!

This is Oz. He was found outside with the feral felines but is the mushiest of CHONKS there is. He loves to smell your breath and SCREAM for the treats. 14/10 would tell Oz I love him until my tongue falls out of my mouth.

This is Roo. She is about 3.5 years old and full of the tortitude. Her interests include: catnip, chasing her sister Cali, catnip, sitting in boxes, and catnip. 15/10 get this angel a strain of the good stuff!

This is Frankie. He is 3 years old and is very silly. His favorite thing is to look at balloons.13/10 Would blow up balloons until I passed out for this sweet boy

This is Mango. She is the most hyperactive cat. She literally gets herself so tired she just flops on the floor and goes to sleep, then when she gets up she's back at it again. She can jump 5ft into the air for a string, and if you throw her a mouse toy she'll pick it up in her mouth and carry it back to you, like a dog. She might have been a dog in a past life. 12/10 Crazy girl. except now she's a cat AND CATS RULE

This is Alice Sunshine. She is a tripod from Serbia. She loves the simple things in life like popsicles and destroying the furniture. 13/10 who needs four legs when your nose is that boopable

This is Gus. Gus is a troublemaker at only a year old. He is sweet and also loves cuddles/being picked up. He's kinda dumb, but in a cute way (like always forgetting to pull his tongue in!). Big ball-o-energy. 12/10 Gus is a MOOD and i love him

This is Liliana. She's a kittenish 13 years old and is quite the lady. Always uses her best manners. 14/10 She can teach these young tom cats a lesson or two

This is Figaro. He is 3, v noisy and bad, but is so loving and adorable.
12/10 it's called balance, hooman.

This is Hopper. He is a one year old bebe and lives in Colorado. He loves to play and being told how cute he is. 13/10 Would die to be able to boop the nose.

This is Lily. She doesn't like other kitties, because she's a attention h o e and she don't care who knows it. 14/10 A beautiful blue eye'd kibbit

This is Tully. She named after her mom's favorite Irish whiskey. She's a five year old Panther Princess who rules the roost. Her favorite things are bird watching from the window, playing with feather toys, and meat tube treats! 14/10 I hate Whiskey but I LOVE Tully

This is Duke Silver. He named after Ron Swanson's smooth, jazz saxophone playing, alter ego His human found him on a cold winter day, now he gets spoiled with tuna on the reg! He also teaches his doggo naughty things like tipping over the trashcans and knocking things off counters. Hopes to rule the world one day. 13/10 N O R T Y boy but v handsome, can do whatever he wants I don't care.

This is Athena. She is a CHONKY goddess of the dilute torties. Spreads love and wisdom and treats. 15/10 Would like to pet the belleh for more wisdom

This is Dominic Melchisadech. He is 13, mostly void and loves food.
He likes people, but is more into sleeping than cuddling these days.
13/10 typical VOID behavior we love it

This is Smokey. He is nearly 5 years old, an avid bird chatterer, biscuit maker, and is superbly chonky. Loves to roll around exposing his belly to poor, unsuspecting hoomans, who cannot resist the urge to rub is voluptuous floof, only to find...IT IS A TRAP! Teef and bunny kicks are his favourite choice of weapons. 15/10 Smokey the sneaky CHONK! Great attack techniques

This is Mittens. He is 4 and sweet and big-boned rescue kitty who is quiet and shy until he gets to know you. After that he'll never stop talking to you! He wants to eat whatever his hoomans are eating, and if he's not getting enough attention while they are sleeping, he'll turn on a light switch to wake them up. 13/10 would have conversations with the house cheeto until my tongue falls out of my mouth

This is Hawking. He is the most hambsomest grey boi who would like you to admire his soul patch. 14/10 and we can't not admire the whiskers while we're here!

This is Ish. She's an older gal from Florida who loves the simple life of laying in the sunshine and giving loves to all of the hoomans. 15/10 WE STAN FOR ISH

This is Lagniappe. She was also born by a dumpster during Katrina, and still has Katrina cough. Blind from her lifelong sinus issues. She will 14 years old on August 29th. 15/10 SHE IS A SURVIVOR SHE NOT GONNA GIVE UP

This is Charli Chunk. She is the Co-owner of #WeRateCats. She really loves belly rubs and treats. If you ask her what she loves more, she would definitely say treats. 15/10 she is truly the sweetest angel on this earth.

This is Herodotus of Halicarnassus. He is 6 and a beautiful long-haired ginger boy. He is very cuddly and madly in love with his hooman dad, to whom he attaches like a limpet. He gets annoyed with hooman for reading instead of paying him attention. 14/10 I don't know how you would do anything else while he is around, would give him my undivided attention 24/7

This is Minnie. She is 2. Minnie loves to supervise all home projects, catch treats with her paws, and gives kisses before going to bed. 12/10 sounds like a hardworking gal. Respect

This is Nova. She is a dainty little angel who has worked really hard to puurfect her tail wrap pose. 15/10 FLAWLESS form baby girl

This is Ms. Griggers. She is also known as Ms. G, iggy cat, and pretty girl. She adopted her hoomans by showing up to their door step. Now she owns the whole house. 15/10 go after ur dreams like Ms. G and you will succeed!

This is Oliver Purris. He's 3 years old, and if you look real close you will actually die of cuteness from his nose freckles. 13/10 would like to boop each freckle at minimum 28 times a day.

This is Gracie. She's turning 11 this year, and she loves wet food and belly rubs. She was found as a very dirty, scruffy, tiny kitten that looked only a couple weeks old. The Vet said she wouldn't survive, but she prevailed! A month later she got out and and two weeks later, her siblings insisted to go out, went straight to the neighbor's porch, and brought her out from underneath. Over the last decade she's only gotten sweeter, cuddlier, and floppier. She's moved states three times and made friends with various dogs and cats. She now lives with her younger sister Tetra, but they still need to work on playing nice. 14/10 this girl is ADVENTUROUS and a queen.

This is Xander. He is 10 months old and is a world-class lounger, even when his sister is busy chasing a moth or some other bug. He likes to lie on his back for belly rubs and seems to think 3:30 in the morning is the best time to receive attention. He's super-sweet and has glorious floof. 13/10 3:30 is a puurfect time for him and what he says GOES, hooman!

This is Pierce and Palmer. They are BROS who enjoy the good c-nip and the good c-nip only. 14/10 would like to squeeze right on in between them for the rest of my days

This is Ulala. She is the best gorl. She is 8 years old and she loves to eat plastic bags and chase hair ties. 13/10 we all got weird cravings and thats ok, when ur this fabulous and floofy you can eat what you want.

This is Callie. She is a goofy tortie who loves to snooze then sprint around the house. 15/10 typical tortitude, we are proud.

This is Frankie. He is is 11 years old and the CFO (cheif feline office) and CEO (cat executive officer) of the household. It's a tough, tiring job but he takes his job as supervisor very seriously. 13/10 GIVE HIMBS A RAISE HE WORKS HARD.

This is Princess Josephin. You may call her Josie. Josie is 2 and a half and was a surprise floof. She had short hair when she was a beeb but a few months later she magically turned into a majestic floof ball who brings her own chonky padding everywhere for maximum comfort. Josie likes to adventure outside and smell all the smells and soak in the sunshine. 13/10 Josie you are a puuuurfect angel

This is Percy and Oliver. They are 2 years old and brothers. While they are a bit chunky, they still play and fight around the house. Sometimes we call Percy "Spartacus" because he almost always "wins" in their little play fights. They are super snuggly and love to nap. 13/10 these house cows are puurfect. Would love to nap with them.

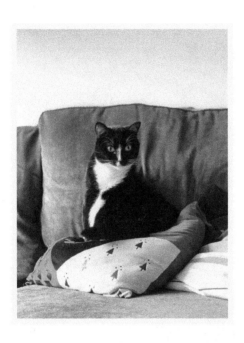

This is Batman. He is 7 and is taking a break from saving the world today. He is exhausted. 12/10 please let him snooze and have a weeks vacation.

This is Sunny Boi and Dmitri. They are in foster care right now, learning to become household CHONKS and work on their litter box skills. 13/10 set your goals boys and you will achieve them!

This is Pippin. His birthday is October 2, 2017. Pip had a rough start to life. Pip lived outside for a little bit as a wild tiger, and did did use up a few of his nine lives. A garage door was accidentally closed on him but he miraculously recovered. He too was attacked by a wild animal, but he was able to escape with only a cut on his head that quickly healed. He also survived a brutal Midwest winter with temperatures as low as -60°F. Finally, a hooman took him in and he's been living the sweet life with an apartment all to himself. Now he sleeps all day, gets food whenever he wants, and never has to worry about anything ever again. 14/10 Pip, you are a LEGEND! You deserve this good life my dude

This is Bo. He is 12. He must get his floof groomed every 4-5 weeks. Loves cat treats. 14/10 You can just tell he is the goodest boy.

This is Gisele. She is trying to watch Real Cats of Beverly Hills and would appreciate it if you could watch your silly news later. Thanks hooman. 12/10 LVP DID IT!

This is Dusty. She's almost two, but she always says she's a wild child and should have been born in the 70's. 15/10 cat-nip & rock and roll is a forever life style

This is Bella. She is 14 years old and does whatever she wants, when she wants. And don't you dare tell her no. 12/10 if I had to guess her astrological sign it would be a scorpio

This is Wednesday and Pugsly. They're in Foster care right now, practicing to be the floofiest of floofs. 15/10 hope they get a home soon cause they're already masters of the floof

This is Treva. She's almost one and has dreams of working in a circus, so she's working on her balancing skills. 13/10 would like to be this house cow's agent when she makes it big

This is Tigger. He 19 years old and a very loving boy, if he's not outside garuntee he'll be laying with someone asleep. For 19 he still lively, sometimes it's as if he runs of duracell batteries. He looks out for his little brother and gives him washes after he's been outside. Definitely a mummys boy. Never fails to welcome me home after work. 14/10 Tigger, you are the SWEETEST BOI EVER. Can definitely see why you're a mummy's boi

This is His Royal Highness King Finnegan Wallace the Third of Hartford upon the Pond. Finn for short. He is a 5 year and was returned from a shelter twice for "not meeting expectations". He's 100% snuggle-loving lap cat and is working on developing his bug catching skills, but sometimes they are scary. He does not like outside adventures and much prefers napping on the couch. He also spends his time avoiding his little sister because, well, little sisters are annoying. 14/10 Finn, you also look so dapper in bowties.

This is River. Kitten life is hard and she is exhausted. Please send her your good vibes that she snoozes well tonight. 13/10 would make a meal out of those pink toe beans

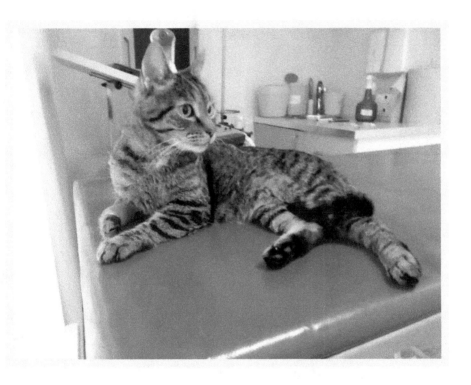

This is Ogis. He is about 10 years old and just had his teefers cleaned. 12/10 Now that they're clean hooman can get the bites for being rude and taking him to the vet, know what I'm saying???

This is Watson. He is 12. He has to sneeze. 14/10 May Simba Bless u, floof!

This is Bartolomea Mosse. She is 3, a tiny void who was found stray on the grounds of a hospital. She is skittish, but loves her hoomans and her siblings. 13/10 STANGER DANGERS Bartolomea! Ur a good girl

This is Oreo. He's about 10 months old. He's mischievous and throws a tantrum if he doesn't get his way. He likes to jump out of windows specially if he can jump onto the back door canopy and scare the sh*t out of his hooman. He makes the doggo cuddle with him too. 14/10 Oreo u is a NORTY boy but soo hambsome plz be careful!

This is Ash. He is a 4-month old tabby from the Philippines. He's sweet and chill but can get super hyper when it's playtime. He obviously loves the camera. 13/10 this boi is b-e-a-utiful!

This is Mr. Tigs, Nora and Luke. Their album drops next year. Still looking for a group name suggestion though. Email us with ideas. 13/10 S Q U A D goals

This is Lola. She is a CHONKY lady who would like to be drawn like one of your french girls. 14/10 Her name was LOLA, she is a CHONKSTER *tune of Copacabana*

This is Gracie. Gracie is a ten year old and has two of those doggo siblings. Gracie started life as a street cat in Harrisburg, PA. One day, she followed her now doggo sister home from a walk. As her canine buddy was waiting to go in the front door, Gracie pushed past her, ran into the house, and has been a spoiled cat ever since. She loves cuddling on her humans and making many biscuits on their laps when a soft blanket is present. At night, she can be found sleeping on her mom's face. 15/10 Gracie knows what she wants and SHE GONNA GET IT!

This is Trammel. He is a billion years old and king of the forest. He sometimes likes the pets, but only for about 4.8 seconds. No more, no less. 15/10 Forever may you reign, white floofy king.

This is Ginny. If you look at her long enough, you will quite literally melt into a puddle from all of her cuteness. 15/10 I would die for this torbie bebe

This is Prince Endymion. He was adopted from Ecuador while hooman was a Peace Corps Volunteer and now currently living in California. He is two years old and enjoys spending his time looking out the window. When he isn't watching the birds pass by the window, he likes to join his hooman while he reads or, just takes naps on the books. 13/10 V educated feline. Should get an honorary doctorate.

This is Winston. He is a chonky house orca who loves to ride on his hoomans shoulder and enjoys a good belly rub from time to time. 13/10 Winnie you are delicious

This is His Royal Highness King Finnegan Wallace the Third of Hartford upon the Pond. Finn for short. He is a 5 year and was returned from a shelter twice for "not meeting expectations". He's 100% snuggle-loving lap cat and is working on developing his bug catching skills, but sometimes they are scary. He does not like outside adventures and much prefers napping on the couch. He also spends his time avoiding his little sister because, well, little sisters are annoying. 14/10 Finn, you also look so dapper in bowties.

This is Charlie and Eli. You mess with one of them, you mess with both of them. 13/10 I've never been more scared yet so in love in my entire life

This is Cammie. She is a year old. You will always hear Cammie purring, because she's the happiest kitty you'll ever meet! She loves to eat, she's a chonk, and cuddle with everyone! She also loves to play fetch. 14/10 would play fetch with her until my arm falls off

This is Callie. She's a year old, loves causing mischief with her sister and climbing high objects. She gets crazy zoomies but at the end of the day her favorite thing to do is cuddle in bed with her hoomans. 15/10 Callie you are an actual A N G E L

This is Damara. She is 2.5 years old and was born with one eye, eyelid was fused to that eye so she had to have it removed. She loves sitting in windows and listening to birds. 14/10 NO EYES NO PROBLEMS

This is Olive. She is a 10 year old spoiled brat. She's a true snuggler. She'll greet me at the door after work and stay by her hoomans side until she leave the next day. 13/10 would be willing to move in so the floofy house cow never has to be alone tbh

This is Oswald. He likes to lay down in weird places. Whenever his hoomans play games he likes to pretend he's playing too. 12/10 he just likes to have fun ok!?

This is Howie. Howie is the prettiest angel ON THIS PLANET.
15/10 HOLY FLOOFING FLOOF GIRL U ARE FLAWLESS

This is Ziggy. He likes to scream and is disgustingly cute. 12/10 would like to boop the house cow's nose on a regularly scheduled basis

This is Boo. She is 8 years old, and you can see how she got her name. 15/10 LAWD I'm scared

This is Lola Phillips. She's an older gal who was abandoned after her owners moved away. New hoomans took her in and she enjoys sleeping on the bed, playing with backscratchers, foods and hiding under Mom's bed. She does not like thunderstorms or fireworks.14/10 lots of wisdom and stories in this girls eyes

This is Waffles. He is 10 months and was nursed back to health when he was found at weeks old. He is doing super well, he now has a great home in southern PA. 14/10 I hope he's living his best life looking cute as a button and getting daily nose boops

This is Eleanor. She was found outside at just 2 weeks old. She's doing very well but yet to be homed. She has one of the most gorgeous coats EVER and a very unique skunk-stripe on her back. 15/10 sweet little angel bebe her future owners will be SO lucky!

This is Chloe and Sophie. They love sleeping together in the sunlight. Chloe is a snuggly, sweet girl who loves all hoomans, and Sophie is a high-energy, playful girl who is a little shy. 12/10 they are Yin and Yang of each other and my heart is crying over it

This is Shrimp Phillips. He's a 3 years old and was adopted after his previous hoomans surrendered him. He's a Hemmingway cat! He has 6 toes on both his front paws. He hasn't stopped purring since he's come home. He loves snuggling, exploring, and napping. 13/10 LEMME SEE THOSE TOE BEANS BOY!

This is Frankie. He is 3 years old and is very silly. His favorite thing is to look at balloons.13/10 Would blow up balloons until I passed out for this sweet boy

This is Ferris. He was found at a state fair when he was a kitten and is now 3. He's always had carnies blood. Slays at the balloon popping game. 13/10 silky smooth house panther VOID

This is Cleo. She's a good, chill girl.14/10 this is one GLORIOUS house orca

This is Pippin. His birthday is October 2, 2017. Pip had a rough start to life. Pip lived outside for a little bit as a wild tiger, and did did use up a few of his nine lives. A garage door was accidentally closed on him but he miraculously recovered. He too was attacked by a wild animal, but he was able to escape with only a cut on his head that quickly healed. He also survived a brutal Midwest winter with temperatures as low as -60°F. Finally, a hooman took him in and he's been living the sweet life with an apartment all to himself. Now he sleeps all day, gets food whenever he wants, and never has to worry about anything ever again. 14/10 Pip, you are a LEGEND! You deserve this good life my dude.

This is Bean. Aka Beanie, Beanie Boots, or Beanie Bug. She is a 2 year old Chunky house panther. Her hobbies include drinking water from the sink (or toilet), stealing her sister's food, and sunbathing. A natural hunter and protector of the hoomans. 12/10 Beanie girl, you own my heart.

This is Rizzo. She was named after Anthony Rizzo from the Chicago Cubs. She is 3. Rizzo is most majestic kitty. She loves meowing for food, reminding the humans to feed her, long naps in the sun, and overeating. Also appreciates a good box. 14/10 she fits perfectly in there CAN'T YOU SEE?!

This is Liliana. She's a kittenish 13 years old and is quite the lady. Always uses her best manners. 14/10 She can teach these young tom cats a lesson or two

This is Basil. He is an adventurous boi who loves to go outside for walks on his harness, playing in toilets, and destroying everything he can. His hooman loves the floof out of him regardless. 14/10 Go hard or go home is Basil's vibe I just know it.

This is Betty. She is no longer with us, but her floof is forever remembered. She liked climbing trees and eating soup. 17/10 Climb high floofy could angel. Always fabulous.

This is Bartek. He is 8 and loves windowsills. He'll trick you for food and chase you around the house. He was adopted as an adult and has so much to give. 13/10 E V E R Y O N E Should adopt, not shop. Senior cats need homes too! also, this blep is AMAZING.

This is Artemis. She was found in -10F on the side of a snowy Alaska road. Loves her toy mouse and warm blankets. Will snatch your Cheez-It crackers if given the chance. 14/10 Artemis and I have a lot in common.

This is Izzy. She is 8 and tries to fight our her pitbull doggo. Spoiler alert: she wins every time. 13/10 LAWD SHE VICIOUS

This is Stella. She's about 6 and a psycho. One minute she's asking for pets, the next she's ripping your hand apart. She enjoys only fresh food from the bag, and can't decide if she wants to be in or out. 15/10 Decisions are hard hooman, back off, ok?

This is Frankie. She is 6 and a bird watching diva. 13/10 love me some chunky loafs

This is Touge. He is 2 and a super cuddly boy. Trouble maker, but only sometimes! He may look SPICY but he is very social. 12/10 I look spicy too but you are deff more social than me.

This is Luna. She is around 3 and the neighborhood outdoor cat. She is super friendly and loves when the hoomans give her wet foods. 14/10 ok wow someone build this girl a house of her own cause she is an independent woman

This is Kitty. He can't meow, but he can squeak. Loves to supervise his hoomans when they're working. 13/10 peep his toe floof

This is Henry and Mimosa. They both just turned 1. Henry likes to steal bracelets and Mims will eat ALL the treats. 15/10 They are partners in crime and quite literally the cutest duo I have ever seen.

This is Vinnie. He was 20 when he crossed over the rainbow bridge. He loved mac and cheese and all of the pets. 18/10 climb high good boy I hope you get the cheesiest of the mac and cheeses up there.

This is Ellie. She is 1.5 years old with google eyes. She begs for baths in the sink. 13/10 she WONKY but hella cute!

This is Finnegan. I don't know why he's in this book. We rate cats, not cows... 13/10 v cute cow tho nice floof.

This is Ferg. He is 2. Ferg loves eating moths and window blinds. His new favorite hobby is hanging out under the bed now that he has succeeded in ripping the liner of the boxspring off completely. 14/10 I'm not even mad at the norty boy, I'm impressed.

This is Zoe. She'll be 17 in January. She can't meow & she's tiny weighing just under 7lbs. She will only eat fresh cat food if it hasn't just been served to her she won't eat it. 15/10 this old gal deserves her food on a gold diamond platter!

Minerva "Minnie" MeowGonagall and Albus "Albie" Dumblepurr. They are brother and sister who love each other very much. Minnie is blind in one eye, so sometimes it's hard to see when her brother comes up to play, but she's a tough cookie. They're about 3 months old and we're rescued from a hoarder's home. They love playing, snuggling, and chasing each other around their new home. 15/10 THEY ARE THRIVING

This is Olive. She is 2 years old, scared of strangers and is super shy. But she LOVES to cuddle with her hoomans. Her favorite toys are the laser and a mouse toy that squeaks. She has a favorite spot to sleep, right by the windowsill in the kitchen 12/10 Olive I would give my life to kiss your nose.

This is Prince Endymion. He was adopted from Ecuador while hooman was a Peace Corps Volunteer and now currently living in California. He is two years old and enjoys spending his time looking out the window. When he isn't watching the birds pass by the window, he likes to join his hooman while he reads or, just takes naps on the books. 13/10 V educated feline. Should get an honorary doctorate.

This is Lily! She is almost 1-year old, loves toys shaped like fish, and was born with feline leukemia. She is loved to the fullest & kept as healthy as possible for as long as possible. 15/10 best blep we have ever seen here at #WeRateCats

This is Jasmine. Her nose is two different colors and she really enjoys loafing. 15/10 If you look up "Puurfection" in the dictionary, her picture is under it.

This is Bartok. Himbs a silky house panther who knows he looks good in purple. 12/10 Purple looks sexy on you, house panther

This is Kramer. She loves water and loves to snuggle her tiny hooman when she sleeps. She is a long VOID and also part bat. 14/10 big K I LOVE YOU

This is Tirzah. She is 11 years old. She used to be a tough street cat but is now a spoiled baby living a life of luxury. 12/10 we love a good floofy under-cat story, respect girl.

This is Penny. She is almost 2 and lives in London. She has a penchant for books, pigeons & feet. 15/10 a torte with an accent is enough to make me combust in happiness OMG

This is Ziggy. He is the youngest in the #WeRateCats household. Ziggy is the FLOOFIEST of floofs. His tail catches all the dust in the house. He loves you, sometimes. 13/10 will try and force him to love me no matter how many scratches it takes

This is Bamboo. He is 4 and has a RCF. *Resting Cat Face* He will accept your pets though, just between the ears. 12/10 Would like to count his toe beans

This is Gingie. He is a softy little cheeto boy is about 10. He is a lil' baby who has the louder purr you could ever hear, an extreme love bug with his big belly who loves everyone who comes round. 14/10 I would walk through boiling hot lava for Gingie

This is Kittie. She's 1 year old and was found dumped in a bush. She absolutely loves to play fetch normally at 6 am and loves her brother so much. She's super hyper and I'm sure she never sleeps. 13/10 NO TIME FOR SLEEP HOOMAN! SHES ONLY GOT 9 LIVES TO LIVE

This is Salem. He is a floofy house panther who loves to love and drinks his water with his paw. 14/10 REGAL A F

This is Luna. She's almost 3. She's a little screamy baby who loves loafing in the garden, chasing small prey, and demanding attention at inopportune times. She also LOVES naps and rolling around in her catnip before eating it. 15/10 I was not aware this is any other way to eat cat nip hmm...

This is Autumn, she is 4 years old. She enjoys going for walks on her leash and if you don't take her out at least three times a day she will make you pay. That face of an angel hides the mind of a powerful monarch. 14/10 Autumn is more beautiful than I will ever be.

CPSIA information can be obtained
at www.ICGtesting.com
Printed in the USA
BVHW062054010320
573703BV00002B/14